Can Balaam's Ass Speak Today?

A Case Study in Reading the Old Testament as Scripture

Walter Moberly

Lecturer in Theology, University of Durham

GW00675086

GROVE BOOKS LIMITED
RIDLEY HALL RD CAMBRIDGE CB3 9HU

Contents

To Jennifer
in wonder and delight

The Cover Illustration is by Peter Ashton

First Impression December 1998
ISSN 1365-490X
ISBN 1 85174 390 1

1

Introduction:
A General Approach to the Old Testament

For many Christians the Old Testament tends to be more of an embarrassment than a resource, more a stone to trip over than a well to drink from. The ghost of Marcion, who in the second century was the first Christian seriously to propose that Christians did not need, and would be better off without, those Scriptures of Israel which came to be known as the Old Testament, still haunts many a Christian mind. Although the official position of the churches down the centuries has been that Marcion was wrong, the actual practice of many churches suggests a position more along the lines of 'he was probably more right than wrong.' Moreover, the level of engagement with the status and role of the Old Testament (in so far as it is engaged at all) often does not rise very much above that of the village atheist—'Science has disproved Genesis,' 'The God of the Old Testament is nasty.' All this is a sign of profound moral and spiritual impoverishment, which will not be overcome without one of the central realities of which the Old Testament itself speaks—a fundamental reorientation of the human heart and mind towards God, classically known as 'repentance.'[1] Towards that larger task this present study is one small contribution.

In terms of approach, there is something to be said for taking a tip from the world of commerce. First we are invited to have a free ride in the new car at the showroom, and see and feel for ourselves what it can do; only then are we invited to discuss technical details (and schedule of payments). Often attempts to formulate some general justification, or principles of usage, for Christian use of the Old Testament do not get beyond preliminaries. So it may be helpful instead to jump in at the deep end and immediately engage with the text.

Such a proposal is, of course, less straightforward than it sounds. Just as top athletes make running or swimming look easy, and one does not see the endless hours of hard training that underlie the performance, so a professional scholar may make biblical interpretation look easy, and one does not see the years of study that make it possible. I do not wish for a moment to deny the hard work that is needed to read Scripture well. But I want to suggest that

---

1   At the time of writing (late September 1998), the recent televised 'confession of sin' by President Clinton, and the general public uncertainty as to how to understand and evaluate such 'repentance' (a difficulty shared, I suspect, by the President), is a reminder of the importance of deepening our moral and spiritual literacy.

the key to good interpretation may lie less in the mastery of technical skills (languages, history, and so on), deeply desirable as such mastery is, than in the basic assumptions and expectations which are brought to the task. Such 'presuppositions' are often formulated in a rather abstract way ('inspiration,' 'infallibility'), which may not convey their true significance. As an alternative way of trying to prepare people to be able to capture the essence both of Scripture itself and of its outstanding interpreters I briefly suggest four presuppositions.

First, the world of the Bible is our world. In saying this I am not discounting the problems posed by the enormous cultural differences between the world of the Bible (which is itself made up of significantly different cultural contexts) and our world today, even though these make precise formulations of shared identity problematic. Rather, I wish to make two affirmations, without which traditional Christian faith cannot function: a) human beings now are the same creatures as then, with the same basic existential realities of life and death and choices of good or evil; b) the God of whom the Bible speaks is the one God, with whom, no less now than then, humanity has to do.

Secondly, the Bible is our own particular story, as Christians. It is not only that humanity generally and God are depicted in the Bible, but, when we become Christians, we discover that the particular story of Israel and Jesus is our story. That is, it is the story of how and why there are at all such people as Jews and Christians in God's world, and what we are here for (though neither 'Jew' nor 'Christian' is the Bible's own preferred way of referring to the people of God, and the easy use of group labels can sometimes obscure that reality of life with God which transcends all familiar and convenient human categorizations).[2] As a child forms his or her identity in a large part through absorption into particular cultures, so we grow as Christians through absorbing a biblical and Christian pattern of thought and life. This is, of course, a prime reason why regular Bible reading, both corporate and individual, so as to 'read, mark, learn, and inwardly digest' the content of the text, is a basic spiritual discipline. Failure to do this means that we grow up deprived, deformed, or amnesiac, never fully appreciating how and why feasting at the Father's table is preferable to eating the pods that pigs eat.

Thirdly, we must read the biblical story with total imaginative seriousness. It is a curious paradox that many people in a culture which does most of its thinking via stories, either the novel or the film, should find it difficult to recognize that the biblical cultures may have operated in fundamentally the same way. Questions of ancient history and textual composition have

2 Compare 1 Corinthians 1.18–2.5.

their place. Too often, however, they actually function to disable rather than enable serious imaginative engagement with the text, by directing attention to questions about the text rather than what the text is about. There is an analogy in the way we may try to disengage ourselves (or others) from uncomfortable tension or suspense in a film by saying 'it's only a film,' 'they're only special effects'; the crunch comes when we know full well all such 'only's,' but we find we are hooked anyway. If we will not read the Bible with at least the same degree of imaginative engagement which we accord to our favourite novels or soaps, no account of biblical authority or reliability is likely to be much more than a form of words.

Fourthly, biblical stories deal with the real, basic and perennial issues of life. Although Christians acknowledge this in principle, in practice the real force of many biblical stories is too easily blunted. On the one hand, we often simply fail to see what the story is about, and content ourselves with focussing on circumstantial details (an abundance of which, often genuinely interesting, present themselves to anyone who works seriously on the biblical text). On the other hand, we think we see the concern of the text, but then either make it sound trite and moralistic, or make every biblical writer sound like a certain popular understanding of St Paul. We need to relearn the discipline of recognizing how in the biblical text the enduring issues of life and death are constantly raised and probed in ways both deep and searching, and how this also makes possible the positive transformation of life today. We best do this—perhaps *only* do this—as we ourselves are willing to open and expose ourselves to God and other people and live truly and faithfully in the way that the Bible envisages.

2
The Story of Balaam and His Ass

The story of Balaam and his ass is a reasonably well known story from the Old Testament. But it is not, I think, one of the best understood. I would like to revisit this famous story and suggest that it may be a good example of how the Old Testament may inform and engage with a contemporary faith. Apart from the intrinsic interest of the story, it also has the advantages of being a case study which displays precisely those Old Testament characteristics to which many people object. On the one hand, theres is a scientific/ historical problem—'How on earth could an ass talk?' On the other hand, there is a moral/theological problem—'Isn't he a nasty God who gets angry and is prepared to kill people?' And the story also has clear implications for a more generalized sense of ideological suspicion, such as is often voiced today—'Isn't the Bible a tool of power play, used by some people to promote themselves at the expense of others?'[3]

The overall story of Balaam in Numbers 22–24 stands as a self-contained unit within the book of Numbers. The summoning of Balaam and his journey prior to his encounter with Balak (Num 22.1–35) is a natural subdivision within the larger story, and this alone will be our focus here.

The King of Moab Summons a Hitman, 22.1–14

¹The Israelites set out, and camped in the plains of Moab across the Jordan from Jericho. ²Now Balak son of Zippor saw all that Israel had done to the Amorites. ³Moab was in great dread of the people, because they were so numerous; Moab was overcome with fear of the people of Israel. ⁴And Moab said to the elders of Midian, 'This horde will now lick up all that is around us, as an ox licks up the grass of the field.'

Now Balak son of Zippor was king of Moab at that time. ⁵He sent messengers to Balaam son of Beor at Pethor, which is on the Euphrates, in the land of Amaw, to summon him, saying, 'A people has come out of Egypt; they have spread over the face of the earth, and they have settled next to me. ⁶Come now, curse this people for me, since they are stronger than I; perhaps I shall be able to defeat them and drive them from the land; for I know that whomever you bless is blessed, and whomever you curse is cursed.'

---

3   The following exposition of Numbers 22 may need further nuance in the light of the Balaam story as a whole in Numbers 22–24 where the peculiar logic of God's choice of Israel, as expressed in Balaam's oracles, cuts against any straightforward moral universality.

The context and issues of the story are deftly set out in these opening sentences. The people of Israel are encamped east of the Jordan in the general region of Moab. Balak, king of Moab, knows of other peoples east of the Jordan whom Israel has already defeated and dispossessed, and is fearful lest a similar fate befall himself and his people. He therefore summons assistance in the form of Balaam, the power of whose curse may enable Balak to overcome the otherwise superior numbers and strength of Israel; for the blessings and curses pronounced by Balaam are, in Balak's view, definitive and determinative. In terms of the narrator's overall perspective and purpose, Balak foolishly supposes Balaam to possess the kind of power of speech which the narrator knows (and as Balak will discover the hard way) no human can possess, but can only be received as a gift from God to those who are faithful.

> *7So the elders of Moab and the elders of Midian departed with the fees for divination in their hand; and they came to Balaam, and gave him Balak's message. 8He said to them, 'Stay here tonight, and I will bring back word to you, just as the* LORD *speaks to me'; so the officials of Moab stayed with Balaam. 9God came to Balaam and said, 'Who are these men with you?' 10Balaam said to God, 'King Balak son of Zippor of Moab, has sent me this message: 11"A people has come out of Egypt and has spread over the face of the earth; now come, curse them for me; perhaps I shall be able to fight against them and drive them out."' 12God said to Balaam, 'You shall not go with them; you shall not curse the people, for they are blessed.' 13So Balaam rose in the morning, and said to the officials of Balak, 'Go to your own land, for the* LORD *has refused to let me go with you.' 14So the officials of Moab rose and went to Balak, and said, 'Balaam refuses to come with us.'*

Senior officials travel on Balak's behalf, to carry out the necessary negotiations to secure Balaam's assistance. Balaam responds as one who speaks for God should respond, in the Old Testament's view of things. He says that he must respond as directed by God—and so, implicitly, does not decide in terms of his own priorities and interests insofar as these might differ from those of God. He also speaks of God with the proper name, YHWH (traditionally translated 'the LORD'), as known by Israel and characteristic of true spokesmen for God (22.8, 13; even though the narrator uses the generic term, 'God,' 22.9,10,12).[4] That night God speaks to Balaam in familiar terms—this is no first meeting or giving of vocation, but a dialogue between those who

---

4 God reveals himself to Moses as *YHWH* ('the LORD') at the burning bush, at Sinai, in an episode that is foundational for Israel's faith, Exod 3.1–4.17, esp 3.13–15.

already know each other.[5] When Balaam explains the situation in response to God's question, God's directive is crisp and clear: Balaam is not to accompany Balak's officials, and he is not to curse the people 'for they are blessed.' So next day, Balaam dismisses Balak's officials, and they return to their master to report their failure.

There is in this paragraph an interesting point of detail, that the officials bring with them 'divinations' (v 7, *qesamim*), the precise meaning of which is disputed. The most common interpretation, predominant in modern translations such as the RSV, and at least as old as the Vulgate, is that of 'fees for divination.' Such a meaning is perfectly plausible, because payment of Balaam is explicitly an issue in the second embassy, at least as Balaam, no doubt correctly, interprets Balak's offer (22.17–18). The Hebrew language, however, has a common word for 'fee' (*sakar*) which one might expect to be used here were that the intended meaning. Also, when Balak makes the offer which Balaam interprets in terms of money, the envoys do not bring the money with them, for the offer is of payment after the job is done (a crucial point in the development of the story).

More likely, therefore, is that 'divinations' means something intrinsic to the practice of divining, that is objects with which divination is carried out, the kinds of things depicted in Ezekiel's vignette of the king of Babylon— arrows, 'domestic idols' (*teraphim*) and liver (Ezek 21.21–23). Whether Balaam would really want or need such objects is beside the point, for the point is that this is what Balak thinks is appropriate. Balak's eager provision of tools of divination is part of the wider contrast in the narrative between the uncomprehending Moabite view of how the divine realm is accessed and the dynamics of prophecy as understood by Israel and as practised by Balaam (who, later in the story, categorically pronounces the futility of divination against Israel, Num 23.23).

Neither Num 22–24, nor the Old Testament more generally, ever offers a definition or account of 'divination' (*qesem*), whose meaning must be inferred from its particular context. Here, Balak's ascription of power to Balaam, together with his provision of divinatory tools, suggests a view of human ability in some way to be in control of the spiritual realm, which lacks both the moral accountability and the sense of contingency of human life before divine transcendence which generally characterize Old Testament prophecy.[6]

---

5   The rhetorical logic of God's opening question, which is not really a request for unknown information (as can be seen from the answer) but which is an appropriate opening gambit to engage Balaam, is similar to that of God's question to Adam in Genesis 3.9, a point of similarity noted by many older commentators, such as the great twelfth century Jewish commentator Rashi.

6   Of course, a clear general distinction between divination and prophecy is not incompatible with recognition that often in practice the distinction may become more or less blurred, and both the Old Testament and subsequent Jewish and Christian faiths provide plenty of evidence for such blurrings.

3
The Testing of a Vocation

[15]Once again Balak sent officials, more numerous and more distinguished than these. [16]They came to Balaam and said to him, 'Thus says Balak son of Zippor: "Do not let anything hinder you from coming to me; [17]for I will surely do you great honor, and whatever you say to me I will do; come, curse this people for me."' [18]But Balaam replied to the servants of Balak, 'Although Balak were to give me his house full of silver and gold, I could not go beyond the command of the LORD my God, to do less or more. [19]You remain here, as the others did, so that I may learn what more the LORD may say to me.' [20]That night God came to Balaam and said to him, 'If the men have come to summon you, get up and go with them; but do only what I tell you to do.' [21]So Balaam got up in the morning, saddled his donkey, and went with the officials of Moab.

Thus far Balaam is a model 'prophet,' for he is accountable and responsive to God, faithfully speaking God's words. The story does not use the prime Hebrew term for 'prophet' (*navi*), but the classic concept of 'prophet' is envisaged. The prophet is *one who speaks for God* (whether about the past, the present, or the future).

If that were all, it could be the end of the story, at least this particular story of Balak's desire that Balaam should curse Israel. It is not, however, for reasons both simple and complex. Balak thinks that Balaam's refusal to come is not a genuine refusal but a negotiating stance; the real meaning of Balaam's words, he thinks, is not 'no' but 'you must offer me more.' So Balak acts accordingly with a more prestigious embassy and an offer that, he supposes, one could hardly refuse, that is, 'name your price, as long as you do what I ask' (vv 15–17).

This provides the first turning point in the story. How will Balaam respond? In the terms of the story Balak sees Balaam as an astute negotiator. One might, however, stand back for a moment and recast the issue in terms related to Balaam's role as one who speaks with God and for God, that is, as a prophet. In various parts of Hebrew Scripture—parts highlighted and affirmed by Jewish and Christian faiths—the responsibility to speak and act for God is presented as a morally demanding vocation, whose full dimensions may sometimes be engendered by an act of divine testing. That is, the person accountable to God finds himself (or herself) in a situation—in divine terms, a situation initiated by God—in which costly demands or difficulties confront him, and in which he must make a renewed, and more searching, affirmative response to his vocation.

An example of such testing of vocation is the portrayal of Joseph in Genesis. To be sure, Joseph's vocation is to be a 'civil servant' rather than a specifically religious figure ('prophet'), but at the climactic encounter with the pharaoh his speech is similar to that of a prophet (Gen 41.25ff). He definitively interprets the mind of God with a message as demanding of practical response (and not just discussion) as any prophetic call to Israel to turn to God ('repent'); and the positive response to Joseph's message averts disaster.[7] Joseph himself is prepared for this vocation through his resisting of temptation and enduring of malice and disappointment (Gen 39, 40). The psalmist's interpretation of Joseph's story in terms of a divine vocation which involves hard testing (Ps 105.16–22, especially 18–19) makes explicit what is consistently implicit in the Genesis narratives.

Thus, in terms of our story, what Balak intends as financial negotiation could also be intended by God as a test of the integrity of Balaam's vocation. How then should one understand Balaam's response to Balak's renewed embassy? The wording of v 18 is impeccably correct: obedience to God is completely non-negotiable, no matter what the inducement to gain. Thus would a true prophet speak. Then in v 19, Balaam's proposes to repeat his nocturnal encounter with the will of God. At first sight, this may seem unproblematic, for it is apparently a repetition of the good practice displayed earlier, seeking God's will rather than following his own preferences. But within this context there are factors which arouse suspicion as to Balaam's motives. First and foremost is the fact that Balaam does not simply dismiss the men. If the words of accountability to God in v 18 are genuine, then they should suffice, for Balaam already knows God's mind with regard to Balak's request and he could dismiss the men without more ado. In particular, the reason given for God's previous refusal to let Balaam go with the initial embassy is not a particular issue of time or circumstance, which might readily change, but a fundamental principle—'they are blessed' (v 12).

The Question of Principle

Whatever the precise nature of Balaam's ability to grasp this principle at this stage in the story (he enunciates the principle of God's blessing of Israel with strong, and increasing, emphasis as the basis of his oracles to Balak when he gets to that point, 23.7–8, 18–20), it remains the kind of axiom that a prophet ought to be able to recognize as such. Moreover, response to such a principle shares the logic of response to divine commandments and prohibitions generally (something which in other contexts is often handled in terms of conscience). If such is the will of God, then obedience is the correct response. The recognition that what counts as obedience may sometimes be

---

7   Compare the depiction of the prophetic vocation in Jer 1.9–10, 18.7–10, Jonah 3.1–4.11.

problematic, and that sometimes divine commandments may point in con-
flicting directions, makes no difference here. For offers of public honour and
financial gain are not the kind of factors that make problematic what counts
as obedience.[8] Rather, they specify the cost of what such obedience might
entail. They create a problem not for the understanding ('Do I know what I
should do?') but for the will ('Am I prepared to do what is right?') and for
the imagination which fuels the will ('Wouldn't vast wealth and reputation
give me what I really want in life?' 'Isn't this a once-in-a-lifetime opportunity?' 'God surely can't want me to be poor and despised').

Thus the fact that Balaam goes again to consult God suggests that he
does not mean what he says in v 18. In other words, Balaam is acceding to
Balak's understanding of his earlier refusal, that it was not a genuine refusal
but a negotiating ploy. He now wants to come with the envoys, because
Balak's offer is one that he 'cannot' refuse. So he wants God to speak again
and say something more, so that he may have the opportunity to accede to
Balak's invitation. (There are resonances with the Mosaic prohibition of 'add-
ing to the word which I am commanding you,' Deut 4.2. The point is about
seeking expedients to evade the cost of obedience, an evasiveness of which
Balaam seems a good example). The language of religious vocation, which
is preserved unchanged, is becoming a tool of self-interested financial negotiation. It is becoming, in a word, corrupt; or, in the terminology of classic
Jewish and Christian interpretation of the story, Balaam is succumbing to
greed.[9]

Balaam's acceptance here of Balak's understanding of his earlier refusal
does of course raise the possibility that that earlier refusal is also to be understood thus by the reader. Such a suspicion, once raised, cannot easily be
confirmed or rebutted, for the text of vv 7–14 is open to either construal. My
judgment of the story as a whole, however, is that the reader should resist
any facile or moralistic tendency to assume that a person who becomes corrupt must always have been so. A moralistic tendency is perhaps the major
weakness in much traditional Jewish and Christian interpretation of the story.
For example, a characteristic Christian reading is that of Charles Simeon,
who says, 'Who that had heard all the fine speeches which he made respect-
ing his determination to adhere to the will of God…would not have con-
ceived him to be a pious character? Yet from beginning to end his conduct

---

8 Similarly, for example, if adultery is wrong, it remains wrong however great the material
inducement. The 1993 Paramount film *Indecent Proposal*, starring Robert Redford, Demi
Moore and Woody Harrelson, is an interesting recent exploration of this issue; although,
characteristically of the time and place of the film (and much contemporary culture), the
nature and significance of 'adultery' is redefined in individualistic and personalist terms
with diminished moral content and no familial or social content.

9 In the interpretation incorporated in the New Testament, the keyword for Balaam's failing
is 'profit'/'gain' (Gk *misthos*, Jude 11; 2 Pet 2.15). In St Augustine's interpretation the
keyword is 'greed' (Lat *cupiditas*, *Questions on the Heptateuch: Numbers* 48).

was a continued course of horrible impiety.'[10] Rather, the text is portraying the more complex situation of the person who is genuinely a prophet (in that he knows and can practise the responsibilities of such a vocation) but who yet may go astray. When a serious divine test, serious because of its genuine allure, confronts Balaam, he wavers from his initial faithfulness to his vocation and succumbs to temptation.

4

The Journey Towards Death — and Life

[22]*God's anger was kindled because he was going, and the angel of the* Lord *took his stand in the road as his adversary. Now he was riding on the donkey, and his two servants were with him.* [23]*The donkey saw the angel of the* Lord *standing in the road, with a drawn sword in his hand; so the donkey turned off the road, and went into the field; and Balaam struck the donkey, to turn it back onto the road.* [24]*Then the angel of the* Lord *stood in a narrow path between the vineyards, with a wall on either side.* [25]*When the donkey saw the angel of the* Lord*, it scraped against the wall, and scraped Balaam's foot against the wall; so he struck it again.* [26]*Then the angel of the* Lord *went ahead, and stood in a narrow place, where there was no way to turn either to the right or to the left.* [27]*When the donkey saw the angel of the* Lord*, it lay down under Balaam; and Balaam's anger was kindled, and he struck the donkey with his staff.* [28]*Then the* Lord *opened the mouth of the donkey, and it said to Balaam, 'What have I done to you, that you have struck me these three times?'* [29]*Balaam said to the donkey, 'Because you have made a fool of me! I wish I had a sword in my hand! I would kill you right now!'* [30]*But the donkey said to Balaam, 'Am I not your donkey, which you have ridden all your life to this day? Have I been in the habit of treating you this way?' And he said, 'No.'*

[31]*Then the* Lord *opened the eyes of Balaam, and he saw the angel of the* Lord *standing in the road, with his drawn sword in his hand; and he bowed down, falling on his face.* [32]*The angel of the* Lord *said to him, 'Why have you struck your donkey these three times? I have come out as an adversary, because your way is perverse before me.* [33]*The donkey saw me, and turned away from me these three times. If it had not turned away from me, surely just now I would have killed you and let it live.'* [34]*Then Balaam said to the angel of the* Lord*, 'I have*

---

10 'Sermon 170,' *Horae Homileticae* II (London: Holdsworth & Ball, 1832) p 132f.

sinned, for I did not know that you were standing in the road to oppose me. Now therefore, if it is displeasing to you, I will return home.' [35]*The angel of the LORD said to Balaam, 'Go with the men; but speak only what I tell you to speak.' So Balaam went on with the officials of Balak.*

I have argued that Balaam is a true prophet who is succumbing to the temptation of financial corruption. But if this is so, God's initial response in v 20 may seem puzzling. Why should God direct Balaam to go with the envoys? Would one not rather expect reference to God's anger, of the kind specified in v 22, and that divine anger would be accompanied at least by a prohibition on going and possibly also by some act of judgment? But the puzzle is clarified by the wider context of the narrative.

First, the whole episode with the ass which follows (vv 22–35) ends with the same divine command to go but say only what God says (v 35a) with which God responds to Balaam's nocturnal enquiry in v 20. At the very point of Balaam's submissiveness to God, where Balaam offers to turn back (v 34), the angel does not, as one might perhaps have expected, say 'go back' but rather 'go on' (v 35). This must mean that whatever the nature of the divine anger and the angelic adversary to Balaam in vv 22–35, God is not simply, *tout court*, opposed to Balaam going to Balak. Balaam's going must in some way represent God's will (the nature of which will become clear in ch 23–24—for God purposes to use Balak's summoning of Balaam in a way that neither of them as yet envisage).

Secondly, when the divine anger is specified and represented in the episode with the ass, the anger takes an unusual and surprising form. One might expect that divine anger would take the form of direct action against the offender, in some such form as afflicting with disease, blinding the eyes, hardening the heart, or even striking dead (all actions of divine judgment attested elsewhere in the Old Testament). In whatever such form it would be immediate and inescapable for the one afflicted, in this case Balaam. Yet the angel with the sword is not like this, for the angel can be, initially at least, avoided. Instead of the angel coming to and at Balaam, the angel is a stationary object which can be circumvented. What this might signify is a matter to which we will return. At present, the important point is the surprising and complex form which the divine anger with Balaam takes in vv 22–35.

In the light of these two factors in vv 22–35, both of which indicate subtlety and complexity in God's anger with Balaam, it becomes appropriate to find some similar complexity in God's initial words in v 20. That is, God's words are not just to be taken at face value as straightforward permission to go, any more than Balaam's pious-sounding words in vv 18–19 are to be taken at their face value as expressing obedience to God (and just as Balak did not take Balaam's initial words at their face value). God tells Balaam the very thing he wants to hear, but it will not mean for Balaam what he may think it will mean[11]—and this is made clear to the reader by the interpretation of God's attitude as one of anger in v 22. In rhetorical terms, God's words in v 20 are ironic. In substantive terms, God's response to the prophet's seeking to corrupt his vocation is to seek to teach him a lesson.

This lesson is the subject of the episode which follows. Recognition of the episode's crafted and drily humorous quality—the highly esteemed and expensive prophet can see less than a proverbially dull animal—and its patterned structure—the threefold encounter with the angel, the two balancing dialogues—should enhance appreciation of its specific meaning, a meaning which is specified through conventions characteristic of Hebrew narrative.

The Angelic Adversary

First, at the outset the angel is said to stand in Balaam's way as an 'adversary' (v 22).[12] The most illuminating parallel to this is in the story of Solomon in 1 Kings. Here, specifically in the context of divine anger with Solomon for unfaithfulness (1 Kgs 11.9), God raises up two particular people, Hadad and Rezon, each to be an 'adversary' (11.14,23) to Solomon. Neither of them defeat or displace Solomon, but each is seen to be an obstacle and irritant to Solomon, and indeed to Israel (11.25), thereby removing the preceding divinely bestowed rest which was characterized by the absence of such hostile irritant (5.4). In significant respects, as Hadad and Rezon are to Solomon, so is the angel with the sword to Balaam: a figure who opposes, dangerous yet without instant or overwhelming implementation of that danger, a figure whose opposing presence symbolizes divine disfavour with the failure in faithfulness of someone who once did, and still should, know better.

Secondly, there is the sequence of threefold confrontation with the angel (Num 22.23–27). The fact that the angel has a drawn sword means that encounter with the angel will be deadly. So when the ass sees the angel, she[13] naturally takes appropriate evasive action, going around the angel rather as one might go around anything hostile or dangerous which is blocking the way in which one is going. This detour irritates Balaam, who expresses his irritation by hitting the ass in such a way as to redirect her. Unfortunately for the ass, the angel reappears, this time in a narrower place where going around is more difficult. Detour is only possible by squeezing through a narrow gap which involves pressing against a wall. This detour not only irritates Balaam but also hurts him, and again he takes this out on his ass. The angel then reappears a third time, in such a narrow place that evasive

---

11 A scriptural parallel would be Psalm 106.15, 'He gave them what they asked for—and sent a wasting disease among them.'

12 Here, and in all the 1 Kings references in this paragraph, the same Hebrew term—*satan*—is consistently used.

13 The Hebrew noun, and related verbs, are all feminine, envisaging a she-ass.

action is no longer possible. So the ass does the only thing she can, stopping and adopting a posture in which she no longer can move. Balaam is now not merely irritated but positively angry, and hits the ass accordingly.

The Dialogues

The ass's attempts to avoid a deadly danger which keeps reappearing in an ever more compelling way evoke incomprehension, anger and violence on the part of the prophet. The scene is set for two dialogues which reveal all—for each dialogue is initiated by a divine action (opening the ass's mouth, opening Balaam's eyes) which enable the truth of the situation first to be expressed and then to be grasped (22.28–30, 31–35).

The ass's first question is a protest at the injustice of Balaam's repeated hitting his ass. The 'what have I done?' means 'what have I done to deserve this?' The ass has thrice saved her master's life, and so should be thanked not maltreated. But to Balaam this is not the case. Because he has seen nothing of what the ass has seen, he sees the ass's behaviour not as saving him but as humiliating him, making him look foolish (v 29a). To crown his incomprehension, he ironically threatens the ass with the very fate of a deadly sword from which she was trying to save them. The first exchange thus underlines the unjust (because ignorant and mistaken) behaviour of the prophet.

The ass's second question pinpoints the failure of the prophet in the very area in which he should excel: discernment, that is seeing and understanding what is going on, especially in relation to God. Specifically, how can the man who cannot interpret the obvious actions of his ass interpret the more difficult actions of God? The ass points to the wholly unprecedented nature of her behaviour. Balaam has had the ass and ridden on her for as long as he can remember with no break up to the present time, and so his familiarity with her patterns of behaviour is as extensive as it could possibly be. So when he is asked whether there is any precedent whatever for her present behaviour (the Hebrew is emphatic, 'have I ever been in the habit of behaving thus?'), he knows full well that the answer is negative and has to say so. The point is that the unusual behaviour should have caught his attention and signified to him that all was not well, particularly when repeated twice more even in the face of his immediate and pain-inflicting expression of displeasure. Such unusual behaviour was obvious both to see and interpret in terms of its general tenor—'something must be wrong.' Balaam's failure to carry out even the simplest exercise of discernment is palpable. His greed has made him blind and foolish.[14]

---

14 Calvin's comments are apt: 'To the great disgrace of the prophet, the glory of the angel was first of all apparent to the ass...Whence came this blindness, but from the avarice by which he had been so stupefied, that he preferred filthy lucre to the holy calling of God?' (cited in C F Keil & F Delitzsch, *Commentary on the Old Testament: I: The Pentateuch* [reprinted Grand Rapids: Eerdmans, 1980] Pt 3, p 169f).

But now that the ass has pointed out his inability to see the obvious implications of her behaviour, there remains a further necessary step. It is one thing to infer from the animal's visible behaviour that all is not well, it is another to see the specific cause and meaning of this behaviour. The ass, having taught Balaam the first part of his lesson, now gives way to the angel to complete it.

When YHWH opens Balaam's eyes, he is able to see what was in front of his eyes, which the ass could already see, the angel standing before him in his way with a drawn, and so deadly, sword (what Balaam sees, v 31a, is depicted identically with what the ass sees, v 23a). Balaam responds in correct manner, with reverent prostration; though whether this action is other than that of a guilty person who recognizes that he is caught by the proper authority is not specified. In any case, what matters is the dialogue, which gives content to, and brings out the meaning of, the encounter.

The angel draws together the two complaints voiced by the ass, Balaam's blindness and injustice, and interprets the meaning of her unprecedented behaviour (vv 32–33). The angel had come as an 'adversary' to Balaam, because there was something unacceptable about the journey he was making. The angel underlines that the ass's actions were not only appropriate but were for Balaam's benefit, for it is only he, not the ass (whether or not the ass realized this), whose life is in peril, for the divine judgment would, significantly, have left the ass unscathed. The angel does not spell out the precise reason why Balaam's course is unacceptable, for in context the reason is obvious as soon as the challenge is made: Balaam is allowing his prophetic vocation to be corrupted by greed, a greed which has made him blind to the presence of the God in whose name he speaks.

These words of the angel, to which we will return, achieve their purpose. They touch Balaam's heart, they bring him to his senses—or, in traditional evangelical terminology, they convict him of sin. Balaam's response (v 34) is one of true turning to God, that is, he repents. First, he unconditionally acknowledges his wrongdoing: 'I have sinned.' Secondly, he acknowledges his uncomprehending inability to see what he should have seen. Thirdly, he expresses willingness to abandon the enterprise that is causing offence; he will relinquish the hoped-for honour and wealth.

Now, however, because Balaam has turned from that which was corrupting his vocation, the angel says that he should indeed continue to go with Balak's envoys. What was a deadly error when undertaken in greed becomes a fruitful course to pursue if done in obedience to God (v 35). The reason for God's direction to Balaam to continue becomes abundantly clear as the story continues in chs 23–24, and has already been hinted at in Balak's initial summons to Balaam: Balaam's ability to bless as well as curse. So Balaam's prophetic responsibility to speak the message of God is repeated, now with the

16

prospect that he will genuinely fulfil his mandate, even though it will not be what Balak wants or expects.

As the story unfolds in Numbers 23–24, thrice an unseeing and obstinate Balak urges on a seeing Balaam, just as Balaam had urged on his ass. Thrice Balaam pronounces blessing on Israel, each blessing with greater length and emphasis. Finally, an angry Balak loses his temper and dismisses Balaam, warning him to leave quickly, and telling him that the God of Israel has deprived him of all he could have expected to receive. Balaam simply replies that obedience to God is more important than unlimited riches (24.10–13). Before departing he offers unsolicited oracles: a long oracle (24.15–19), which climaxes in a victorious leader for Israel who will defeat many, Moab first of all (24.17b), and some brief visions of glory and disaster for other peoples near to Israel (24.20–24)—the kind of visions appropriate to one who has learned to discern God's will as Balaam has.

A Context for Discernment

To conclude the basic exposition, it may be helpful briefly to stand back from the story and to reflect further on the peculiar nature of the angel's opposition to Balaam—the potentially deadly adversary who can initially be circumvented (for he only takes his stand on the road that Balaam is taking), but with whom an encounter is ultimately inescapable. What is the significance of this particular expression of divine anger?

An analogy may perhaps prove helpful.[15] Consider an active man (or woman) who begins to have health problems. Where previously he had been able to push his body to do more or less what he wanted, his body starts to function differently and to display symptoms that it had never displayed before—breathlessness, vertigo, sharp pains, or whatever. The man knows his body and its previous capabilities, so how should he interpret these unprecedented symptoms? He might decide (perhaps with appropriate medical advice) that his bodily symptoms are warning signs of potentially dangerous overload and that he can no longer do what he did before, and so he begins to modify his activities so that his body returns to normal. But he might decide to ignore the bodily symptoms, dismissing them as a mere passing irritant of no real significance. Suppose he is in the middle of an important project, which needs his full energies. So he makes the latter decision, and continues to push himself as previously. After a while, the symptoms recur, in more acute and prolonged form. He faces the same choice as before. His important project is still his first priority, and so he continues to

---

15 My analogy has obvious resonances with the famous designation, ascribed to St Francis of Assisi, of one's body as 'Brother Ass,' but the analogy is intended as a genuine analogy and not a covert allegory (although sometimes the distinction between analogy and allegory may become blurred).

ignore the symptoms and pushes on. A few days later he has a major heart attack and drops dead.

The analogy is to help us think more about a situation where there are warning signals which, while clear on one level, are such that they can be misunderstood and ignored if their obvious *prima facie* significance conflicts with other priorities. For some priorities, especially those which promise advancement of one's own interests, may make one heedless of more humble alternatives. But what is needed, when a body begins to display problematic symptoms, is careful discernment to find out what they are symptoms of. On the one hand, one must attend to the precise nature of the symptoms, and on the other hand one needs a wider knowledge of the body and health such that the symptoms can be rightly located and understood.

So too, I suggest, Balaam's predicament with the angel requires not only attention to the ass's unusual behaviour but also a wider knowledge, a frame of reference, rightly to locate and understand that behaviour. Within the context of the story that frame of reference is not some form of ancient Israelite zoology but rather Old Testament prophecy. The story is a story of a prophet who succumbs to temptation by corrupting his prophetic vocation through ambitious greed. Balaam's problem is in essence a moral and spiritual failure. God's anger, and the adversarial appearance of the angel, are the counterpart to that failure, to be understood in the moral and spiritual categories of prophecy.

Specifically, the angel with the deadly sword represents the moral and spiritual responsiveness of God to Balaam's self-seeking, with all the two-edged nature of divine encounter, whose outcome is not determinable apart from the human response to that encounter. On the one hand, the angel means death if Balaam persists in the way he is going, for the corruption of prophetic vocation is a course that leads to death. The deadly nature of Balaam's corrupting is not instant and obvious, for the angel may initially be circumvented and the angel does not pursue Balaam. However, the angel reappears always in the very way in which Balaam is going, and the initial possibility of detouring while still remaining on course is progressively removed. Ultimately, there is no avoiding death on that particular road—though death would only strike the one who is choosing to go that way, and the innocent animal would remain unscathed. On the other hand, there is the possibility of repentance and a transformation of Balaam's mission, a possibility initiated by actions of divine mercy (opening the ass's mouth, opening Balaam's eyes), for Balaam in his greed has become blind. This mercy humbles Balaam by confronting him with his utter incompetence and showing him how close to disaster his quest had brought him. But this mercy also teaches him the necessary lesson when he acknowledges his sin, and so enables him to go and speak as a prophet should speak.

5
Balaam: Saint and/or Sinner?

This rich and subtle story raises many further issues which deserve some comment. I will focus on one: the well-known problem of the character of Balaam, a problem that might be posed as 'Balaam: Saint and/or Sinner?' Within the story of Numbers 22–24 there is the obvious tension between the person who succumbs to greed, with whom God is angry, and the person who speaks God's words to Balak in poetic oracles which glowingly depict God's delight in Israel, one of the prime depictions in the Old Testament of God's 'election' of Israel. If the episode of the ass is understood as above then this tension is not a real problem: Balaam is a true prophet who 'falls from grace' but is restored.

However, the picture is complicated by the references to Balaam beyond the story, in Numbers 31. In a campaign against Midian the Israelites kill Balaam (31.8), and Moses says that Balaam was responsible for Israel's apostasy at Peor (31.16), an apostasy related in Numbers 25 immediately after the Balaam story of Numbers 22–24. Balaam the true, though fallible, prophet (Num 22), and Balaam the inciter to apostasy (Num 31)—Balaam, saint or sinner?

The predominant tendency among Jews and Christians down the ages has been to combine the portrayal of Balaam in Numbers 31 with that moment in Numbers 22 when he succumbs to greed, and also, in the light of Moses' words in Numbers 31.16 to make a substantive (effect and cause) linkage between the apostasy of Israel in Numbers 25 and the story of Balaam which precedes. That is, Balaam has been seen as a consistently negative character, a deceptive figure, for whom the episode with the ass (whose actual significance has often received little attention) is solely mockery of his pretensions (and not also merciful correction of his error). His speaking truly to Balak must thus be understood as an act of divine grace, unconnected with, and overruling, Balaam's own character and intentions. And his initial dismissal of Balak's envoys must be seen as Balak saw it, solely as a negotiating stance.

The logic of such an interpretation is clear. The categorical statement of Num 31.16 and the clear implication of Num 22.15–22 make for an overall assumption about Balaam which causes a rereading of other material that appears to portray him more positively. Gordon Wenham, for example, offers a lucid example of this train of thought in his valuable Numbers commentary. In the light of the problem posed by Numbers 31 he suggests: 'The deeds of Balaam which many commentators construe so positively might have a more sinister meaning. The constant harping on money matters might suggest that Balaam's apparent indifference was really an oblique demand for a huge fee (*cf* Gen 23.11–15). The repeated statements that Balaam will declare only the word that God puts in his mouth may be intended to emphasize the inspiration of the oracles rather than the holiness of his character.' Thus 'the author of Numbers 22–24 did not intend to portray Balaam as a saint' and 'he had a poor opinion of Balaam's character.'[16]

This solution, however, creates two problems. One is that it founders on the plain sense of Numbers 22 (and 23–24), as I have tried to set out above. The other is that it presupposes a dubious understanding of the action of God within a human mind. Even on a positive understanding of Balaam as a true prophet, his oracles about Israel are a gift of grace that transcend the limitations of normal human understanding. But to suppose that God's grace in the oracles so overrules Balaam's understanding that he utters that which he himself not only does not believe but is opposed to, is to invoke a mechanistic and manipulative model of grace which has no foundation in Scripture or in Christian faith.

Of course, it is fundamental that God can overrule human intentions and bring good where people intend bad (as in the story of Joseph and his brothers, Gen 50.20, and supremely in the passion of Jesus, Acts 2.23). And Caiaphas can utter words of whose deeper truth he cannot begin to conceive (Jn 11.45–53). But in all such cases the people genuinely mean what they do and say, and the divine grace resides in a transformative power which is operative at the time of the evil actions and words but can only be discerned by the wise and faithful eye subsequently (even though one may trust at the time of the evil action that God is working for good in ways that one cannot see). It is the supposition that there is a palpable, in principle discernible at the time, conflict between Balaam's intentions (hostile to Israel, resistant to God) and his words (favourable to Israel, obedient to God), because of divine overruling, that introduces a model of divine action that is false to the biblical witness to the nature of both God and humanity. In essence, it replaces the Spirit with schizophrenia.

How then should the disparity between Numbers 22 and Numbers 31 be understood? Most modern commentators offer the equivalent of a shrug of the shoulders. There are simply disparate traditions contained within the Old Testament. It is the task of scholars to recognize and describe these traditions in their disparity, and to offer informed conjectures as to why such disparities might have come about and have been preserved. To try to reconcile or harmonize that which is patently disparate is futile. But while there may be justice in such an approach as an exercise in ancient history, it is

16 *Numbers* (Leicester: IVP, 1981) pp 167,168.

difficult not to feel that the canonical presentation of the material requires some fuller grappling with the issue. I offer three suggestions.

First, living and working with tensions can be productive, for they dispel superficiality and complacency. To work at the tension between 'saint and/or sinner' can lead to a deeper engagement both with the miracle of grace and with the depths of human sin. A fine example is Bishop Butler's early 18th century sermon, 'Upon the Character of Balaam,' based upon the text of Numbers 23.10, 'Let me die the death of the righteous, and let my last end be like his.'[17] Although one can point to deficiencies in the sermon in exegetical terms,[18] Butler engages with the big biblical issues in a way that highlights the triviality (amidst technical expertise) of so much scholarly biblical commentary. Let me try to convey the feel of Butler's treatment by quoting what he says about 'saint and/or sinner':

'So that the object we have now before us is the most astonishing in the world: a very wicked man, under a deep sense of God and religion, persisting still in his wickedness, and preferring the wages of unrighteousness, even when he had before him a lively view of death [sc Num 23.10], and that approaching period of his days, which should deprive him of all those advantages for which he was prostituting himself; and likewise a prospect, whether certain or uncertain, of a future state of retribution: all this joined with an explicit ardent wish, that, when he was to leave this world, he might be in the condition of a righteous man. Good God, what inconsistency, what perplexity is here! With what different views of things, with what contradictory principles of action, must such a mind be torn and distracted! It was not unthinking carelessness, by which he run on headlong in vice and folly, without ever making a stand to ask himself what he was doing: no; he acted upon the cool motives of interest and advantage. Neither was he totally hard and callous to impressions of religion, what we call abandoned; for he absolutely denied to curse Israel. When reason assumes her place, when convinced of his duty, when he owns and feels, and is actually under the influence of the divine authority; whilst he is carrying on his views to the grave, the end of all temporal greatness; under this sense of things, with the better character and more desirable state present—full before him—in his thoughts, in his wishes, voluntarily to choose the worse—what fatality is here! Or how otherwise can such a character be explained?

---

17 The edition to which I have access is W E Gladstone (ed), *Butler's Works: Vol II: Sermons* (Oxford: Clarendon, 1896) pp 121–135.
18 Butler wholly ignores the episode with the ass and draws in a traditional way upon Numbers 31, and so supposes that Balaam's succumbing to temptation in response to the second embassy still characterizes his disposition in his encounter with Balak.

21

'And yet, strange as it may appear, it is not altogether an uncommon one: nay, with some small alterations, and put a little lower, it is applicable to a very considerable part of the world. For if the reasonable choice be seen and acknowledged, and yet men make the unreasonable one, is not this the same contradiction; that very inconsistency, which appeared so unaccountable?...'[19]

Butler reminds us of the enduring value, in terms of moral and spiritual insight, of much premodern biblical study, although for most of us today it is indeed a buried treasure.

Secondly, an imaginative holding together of the differing portrayals of Balaam must resist trying to find warrant for Balaam the seducer in Numbers 22–24, but rather see Numbers 31.16 as presupposing another story about Balaam which has not been preserved, but whose imaginative location lies between the end of Numbers 24 and the beginning of Numbers 25. The force of this would be that the true prophet of Numbers 22–24, who was for a while seduced by temptation but who was restored to speak with powerful insight about Israel and God—a story about the power of God's grace—was on a subsequent occasion seduced without restoration and entangled Israel in his own downfall. It would be a monumental turning away from God, a terrible warning along the lines of 'let anyone who thinks that he stands take heed lest he fall' (1 Cor 10.12). The only trouble is, the key narrative is not in Scripture and is entirely an inference.

Thirdly, the problem posed by the different portrayals of Balaam should not be considered in isolation from a similar problem posed by differing portrayals of Israel. That is, in Numbers 22–24, the depiction of Israel in Balaam's oracles (three solicited, Num 23.7–10, 23.18–24, 24.3–9, and the final one unsolicited, 24.15–19) is glowing—the people in whom God delights, in whom God 'sees no trouble' (23.21), and to whom God gives strength and victory. Yet elsewhere in Numbers Israel is more or less consistently unfaithful and rebellious, and the apostasy at Peor epitomizes Israel's general disposition. This is the prime problem of 'saint and/or sinner' which Numbers 22–24 poses. When all is said and done, we are left with an enduring paradox and tension, in one form or other, between the definitive call of God and gift of grace, on the one hand, and the enduring sinfulness and only intermittent faithfulness of God's people, on the other hand. It is within that paradox that we as Christians still live today.

---

19 'Balaam,' p 128f.

6
Conclusion:
Understanding and Using the Old Testament Today

I have tried to expound the story of Balaam and his ass in such a way that its meaning and significance is, I hope, clear. With such stories any application should be intrinsic to the understanding of the story. As with many of the parables of Jesus (or stories or plays more generally), application is not, or should not be, primarily a matter of drawing out further points or morals in some form other than that of the story. To draw some abstract or general moral, such as 'we should not be greedy,' adds nothing to the story and indeed detracts from it, for it is weaker in every way than the biblical text. Such moralizing implies that the content of the story is separable from the fact that it is a story, and entirely fails to recognize the power of narrative and of the imagination.

To be sure, many questions may yet be asked of the text. But such answers as can usefully be given must not suddenly undercut or abandon the text. So, for example, the 'Isn't God nasty?' objection can without too much difficulty be seen to rest on a failure to grasp the moral and spiritual seriousness of encounter with God as portrayed by the text. That decisions and actions might have life and death consequences is a thought that is unpalatable to many. But (if we are wise) we read Scripture to discover the truth about God and our human situation, which may often mean learning to come to terms with that which initially appears unpalatable.

The 'how can an ass talk?' objection also looks different when the contours of the story have been grasped. Of course, debate about the possibility and meaning of miracles is a real and significant debate in every age. But is it really the issue here? For example, St Augustine's comment on the story, that if Balaam had not been so carried away by greed he would have been terrified by such a portentous miracle,[20] in fact only underlines that within the story the ass's speaking is not a problem, at least not in those terms. The speaking is a gracious action of God, but the significance attaches to what the ass says rather than to any supposed marvel that the ass should speak at all (just as it is what the serpent in Eden says, rather than its speaking at all, that is remarkable). To put it differently, biblical writers may use devices and techniques similar to those used by many novelists and filmmakers, techniques designed to aid understanding of and engagement with the story

20 *Questions on the Heptateuch: Numbers* 48.

(as, for example, Luke's depiction of the great drops of sweat on Jesus' brow in Gethsemane (Lk 22.44) is the narrative equivalent of a zoom lens, bringing the reader into intimate proximity to Jesus' struggle). If such devices do not convey a sense of what is true, then they fail. But the recognition of their truth is part of a complex reality which is not dependent upon any simple correlation with some hypothetical detached observer's account of what might have 'really happened.' To say this is not to encourage credulity towards the doubtful and the fraudulent. It is to insist that those criteria by which the truth of stories is recognized (or appropriately denied) are more rich and subtle than the impatient and the cynical are likely to appreciate.

To conclude. The purpose of good commentary on, and exposition of, the text of Scripture should be to leave ourselves not with something other than that text, but rather with the text itself better understood and better able to be appropriated. For it is in and through the words of Scripture that we especially expect the Holy Spirit to speak to us and to direct and shape our lives.